Ancient
L.A.

and other essays

by Michael Jacob Rochlin

**Unreinforced
Masonry
Studio**
Los Angeles

This book is printed on partially recycled paper.
Typeset and printed in the United States of America.

Published by
Unreinforced Masonry Studio
P.O. Box 33671
Los Angeles, CA   90033

Book Design by Hal Taylor.
Cover Design by Randall Tinear.
URM building plan information provided by Peter Quentin, Structural Engineer.

Rochlin, Michael Jacob
Ancient L.A.
ISBN# 0-9648304-1-8   CIP#99-093712
1. Architecture--California--LosAngeles.
2. History--California--Los Angeles Region.
Architecture-Los Angeles 3. Cities and Towns Planning--Los Angeles. I. Title.

To the memory of Carol

Fig. 1

And The Trees Were Very Tall

On the night of February 7, 1998, in the middle of an El Niño downpour, having lived over one thousand years, its innards eaten away by fungus, the Louise Avenue Giant fell over dead. [1] Tended to, or at least left alone, by half a dozen passing societies, one of the oldest and mightiest oaks in the state could quite simply stand us no longer.

Like an ailing oak, our city is full, broad and shaky. Misguided beliefs about the urban future have made an unsustainable urban present. We are called, a "Modern City;" we are not. An "Instant City," the "City of the Future;" we are neither. Degraded for our vapidity, boostered for our beauty, we remain the misunderstood brunt of critics and the misrepresented nostalgia of romanticists:

"Long ago, in a strange country by the Western Sea, a golden sun cast its bright beams upon silver water in a tiny stream flowing beside rounded hills.

"Loneliness lay upon the land.

"Neither horses nor cattle were known here. Only deer and rabbits and doves and quail drank from the stream. This county was waiting for a name, for as yet it had none.

"It was bound by a spell of enchantment. For a thousand centuries, it had basked under the benevolent sun, quickening in the spring to greenness upon its hills and drowsing in the brief winter to the lullaby of rain borne upon gentle winds. It was waiting for a destiny in the unknown, but there was no hurrying in its vigil.

"Then out of curiosity and legend in a far-away place called Spain, where exploration was a burning fire in the veins of a thousand mariners seeking the fabled route to the Indies, a name was given to the undiscovered country which as yet existed only in the imagination of civilized man.

"California.

"And, as discovery neared, the stream beside the hills became marked by Providence upon the map of Fate as the site of one of the strangest settlements in the history of mankind's wandering upon the face of the globe."[1]

*

"Los Angeles provides a massive culture

shock for those Easterners who believe that life ends west of the Hudson River. Angelenos are sometimes portrayed by them as living on the outskirts of a vast wasteland, as persons of little couth, who are culturally vapid; tending toward a laid-back life spent in hot tubs."[2]

*

"'Agua! Agua! Agua!'

Through gray alkali dust that silvers their bare brown feet, the Indians walk through the dazzling white sunshine of the summer afternoon in the lazy pueblo of Los Angeles."[3]

In limbo between iconoclastic paradise and vulgar wasteland, we commuter frogs ponder our pond atop freeway frying pans. Are we ancient Jericho—building a wall bctween desert strangers and our spring water and hybrid grain? Are we Monejo-Daro—wiping our feet as bubbling mud rises yearly in our streets? Arc we Pompeii—grabbing our gold coins as volcanic ash encases our bodies? No, we are "Modern," "Instant," "Futuristic" Los Angeles—caught in traffic, staring at billboards, wondering about home. We are "Sunny" L.A., shoveling coal into the furnace of our fated system, breathing the smog, blind to the delicate, life-giving terrain beneath our feet.

What is Los Angeles? What is its structure? Where are its patterns? How did it grow? Journey through three basin essays: the first, uncovering the origin of our organization of lines and grids; the second, searching for our center, real or imagined; the third, discussing our repetitious order.

*

1Ed Ainsworth, *Enchanted Pueblo-Story of the Modern Metropolis Around the Plaza de Los Angeles* (California: Bank of America, 1959).

2Andrew Rolle, *Los Angeles-From Pueblo to City of the Future* (San Francisco: Boyd & Fraser, 1983).

3Boyle Workman and Caroline Walker, *The City That Grew* (Los Angeles: Southland Publishing, 1935).

Ancient L.A.

and other essays

And the trees were very tall,
And there were no streets at all,
Not a church and not a steeple-
Only woods and Indian people.

excerpt from "Indian Children"
by Annette Wynne

Fig. 1

Ancient L.A.

Two hundred feet above the crashing Torrance surf, a swimming pool sits unused through the night, its waters illuminating the condominium walls an eerie blue-green. [1] On the grounds of the San Gabriel Mission, a cactus grows through its supporting wood slat trellis. On the outskirts of downtown, a roadside plaster statue wears a cracking painted checkered shirt and holds a black tire in each of its giant hands. In Inglewood, water trickles down the side of a drinking fountain while in Wilmington, a parrot lies dead in the grass and a run-over cat looses its shape decomposing into the asphalt of Pacific Coast Highway.

Why is our city the way it is? Why did it grow the way it grew? What holds it together (or keeps it from falling apart)? Manhattan has its grid; Paris, its axes; Bei-Jing, its central Forbidden City—all we have in Los Angeles is a puzzle. From an airplane, one may speculate

Fig. 2

that like other American cities, we are a product of the industrial revolution, a modern extension of Roman planning. Driving into town, however, one might decide that we are a linear city, a system of freeways, a seemingly endless series of lanes. Maps emphasize different qualities, but satellite photos show a flat gray texture surrounded by mountains and bordered by ocean. What is the origin of this challenge to nature? How is this seemingly endless spread organized? How to comprehend a gray presence so large, so overwhelming, yet still considered one place?

Rocketing into the future, we can lose touch with our past. Our technology now allows us to look at ourselves from several miles above the earth's surface, but can we confront what lies thirty-six feet below it? This is Malaga Cove [2-3] the site of the most ancient known settlement in the county. Four well-defined levels of inhabitation were found under this very expensive property, the oldest, bottom-most layer dating back at least seven and possibly tens of thousands of years. Artifacts from the top layer of Malaga Cove indicate a culture only just over a thousand years old—a culture which produced excellent baskets, canoes, nutritious foods, that rarely conducted war, maintained a stable systems of laws and government, conducted marriages, initiation rites, funerals and other religious ceremonies, and also maintained a sophisticated system of villages and paths.

In comparison to this extended duration, Old World influence on our area seems like an eruption rather than the growth of a major city. Found at Malaga, immediately under the eight feet of overburden, at the top of the uppermost layer of gray sand, less than two hundred years old, were deposits of cheaply made glass trade beads. As at sites throughout the county, this indicates the end—the uprooting and subsequent decimation of the indigenous population, the formation and growth of a predominate urban center [4], the establishment and development of outlying towns [5], the spreading [6] and eventual melding of satellites and center into one all encompassing pattern, and of course, the encroachment upon and eventual covering of ancient sites such as Malaga Cove.[1] [7]

Partly because of this explosive growth, Los Angeles has been labeled an anomaly—different than other U.S. cities—its urban plan not conforming to East Coast and European centralized prototypes. Traditionally, historians have painted a convenient picture of a small Pueblo growing into an expansive grid.[2] Post-World

Fig. 3

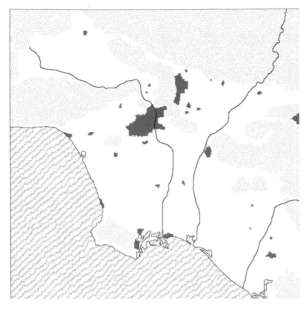

1900   Fig. 4

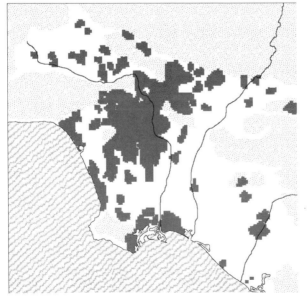

1925   Fig. 5

16

Fig. 6   1950

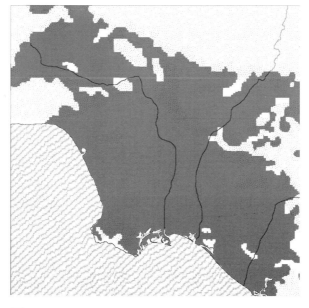

Fig.7   1975

17

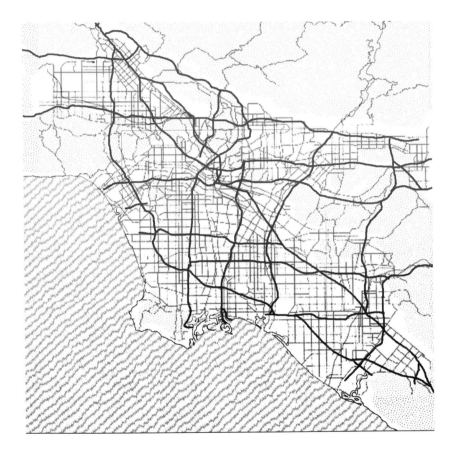

Fig. 8

War II decentralization inspired another description. Writers disregarded the center and focused instead on huge subdivisions interconnected by lines of mass transit.[3] More recently, theorists have attributed Los Angeles' "extended, open, unbounded matrix" to American capitalist origins, citing its unique character and "decisive departure from European models."[4] Yet even with three basic theories to choose from, we are left with fundamental questions about the city's underlying structure; its placement of commercial centers, its choice of lines of communication, its relation to the landscape--the intrinsic features, elements and characteristics that together form an invisible layer. An organic layer so seamlessly integrated that it is not seen by the contemporary eye—so seamlessly integrated that a review of the history of Los Angeles' growth reveals but a shadow of its surprisingly consistent patterns. Los Angeles is both unlike and just like other American cities—a composite of lines and grids, laid over the landscape, two distinct organizations, pushing and pulling, expanding and contracting, yet still married and inseparable. [8]

Although associated with the new freeways, the linear organization is actually the older of the two. The placement of settlements and system of roads throughout the county was based on the original network of indigenous villages and trails. [9] To exploit labor, Missions and Pueblo were located in proximity to these villages. After villages had been depopulated, ranchos were located on these choice and desolate sites. Subsequently, small cities and boom towns were built on top of those. Trails connecting the villages and other significant sites became roads, then highways, then freeways.

The local grid system grew from numerous locations but predominantly from the pueblo center. When the freeways emboldened the linear system in the middle of the twentieth century, the air was let out of downtown dominance. Simultaneously, the empty areas between compass, quarter-compass and coastal grids were bridged with in-fill sewing together and strengthening the overall grid organization, unifying this expanded collection of residential, commercial and industrial zones.

Now, the lines, whether ancient or contemporary, no longer only connect distant settlements but also provide a system of navigation through a patchwork of melded incorporated and unincorporated cities. Although these elements are present in other U.S. cities, the exaggerated size and scale of Los Angeles' all encompassing pattern is what has drawn recent attention and what is seen as representing some-

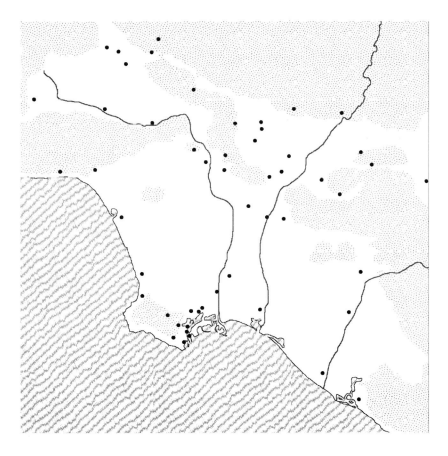

Fig. 9

thing new or different.

The hybridization of indigenous and western systems at this scale is rare and this is not without reason. The collision between Western European and Indigenous Southern Californian cultures delivered an impact from which we are still reeling. Spanish military and religious administration, Mexican feudal leadership and American profiteers demonstrated little comprehension, much less appreciation for the generously-spaced composition of indigenous villages.

For thousands of years, our region's population had remained decentralized, divided into "tribelets."[5] The largest grouping of tribelets was located by the natural harbor, lakes and estuaries of San Pedro and Wilmington. Harbor village locations vary from source to source. Tsavingna may have been near the original town of San Pedro; [10-11] Xujungna, on the shore below the bay; Ataviangna, below Xujunga and Munikangna on the small hills further north.[6] Tovemungna was possibly in the White's Point-Royal Palms vicinity, while Kingkingna and Harasgna were further south and most likely related to the Channel Islands.[7] A very large kitchen midden was discovered along Gaffey, and the largest village, Suangna, is traditionally placed in the area of Harbor Lake. [12-20]

Fig. 10

Fig. 11

Fig. 12

Fig. 13

Fig. 14

Fig. 15

Fig. 16

Fig. 17

Fig. 18

Fig. 19

Fig. 20

Fig. 21

It is easy to imagine Suangna Village and its sister Mausuangna practically anywhere around the perimeter of this natural lakeside preserve. There is to this day even a corner park [21] that was once dedicated to it.[8] Ironically, however, most sources place the Suangna Village site on the grounds of what is now arguably the biggest eyesore in the city—the Union Oil refinery plant.[9] [22-24]

Tragic as it may seem, this crude transformation is fairly representative of post-contact tendencies. As early as the late eighteenth century, San Pedro had established itself as Los Angeles' principal harbor. In 1784, the harbor villages fell under the Rancho San Pedro land-grant becoming the area's first rancho.[10] Suangna became a large (coerced labor work farm) *rancheria*. In 1822, the area became Mexican territory and by 1846 the Mexican government set much of it aside as a reserve. By then, exploitation and disease had decimated the native population and only remnants of the village still existed.[11] Los Angeles soon after became US territory and by 1868 San Pedro was connected to Los Angeles by the Southern Pacific Railroad.[12] The U.S. military took over the Mexican reserve, there were harbor improvements by 1877, and San Pedro was incorporated into the City of Los Angeles in

Fig. 22

Fig. 23

Fig. 24

Fig. 25

1909. Oil was discovered in this area after World War One, and wartime housing and other projects filled in its compass grid during World War Two. Construction of the 1 10 Harbor Freeway began in the 1950's.

This represents the typical local pattern for early growth. For proximity to sources of forced labor, Missions and Pueblo were placed adjacent to Indigenous Villages. Ranchos reoccupied the desolated sites. Boomtowns replaced ranchos. Grids filled-in open space and melded with adjacent grids. [25]

Another coastal example of this pattern is Redondo Beach. [26-27] Engnovagna was located near the "Old Salt Lake," an indigenous source of salt.[13] Disease, forced labor at the Missions and evictions obliterated the area's indigenenous population. With early nineteenth century land grants, these sites fell under the domain of the Mexican Rancho Sausal Redondo. A salt works was erected in the 1850s, the city of Redondo Beach was founded in 1881, and the Santa Fe Railroad built a line to the town in 1888.[14] Redondo became a stop along the Pacific Electric Railway which together with the town's main thoroughfare, Pacific Coast Highway, trace portions of the Old Salt Road. Hopes for a major harbor never materialized, Redondo's coastal grid [28] even-

Fig. 26

Fig. 27

Fig. 28

Fig. 29

Fig. 30

tually melded together with surrounding cities and the San Diego Freeway plowed through in the early 1960s. The AES Corporation Redondo Beach Generating Station today occupies the site of the Old Salt Lake. [29-30]

A well-known inland city that follows this pattern is Whittier, once called Sukagna, "place of wild bees."[15] The Portola Expedition, following trails connecting villages, passed through in 1769. In 1771, the village fell under Mission San Gabriel, the trails becoming branches of the *El Camino Real*. Sukagna villagers were forced to became servants on Rancho Los Nietos.[16] The land changed hands several times, and by the time the Quaker organization, the Pickering Land and Water Company founded the town in 1887[17], the indigenous settlements as well as the ranchos were gone. Although a college was established in 1891 and the city was a stop along train and trolley routes, the area remained fairly agricultural. By the time the path of the adjacent 605 Freeway followed the San Gabriel River to Long Beach (were there were formerly three indigenous villages), Whittier's farms were gone and its compass grid had already intermeshed with surrounding cities. [31-40] So consistent is this pattern [41-42] that a majority of Los Angeles County towns with a 1900 pop-

Fig. 31

Fig. 32

Fig. 33

Fig. 34

Fig. 35

Fig. 36

Fig. 37

Fig. 38

Fig. 39

Fig. 40

Indigenous Villages (partial)   Fig. 41

50

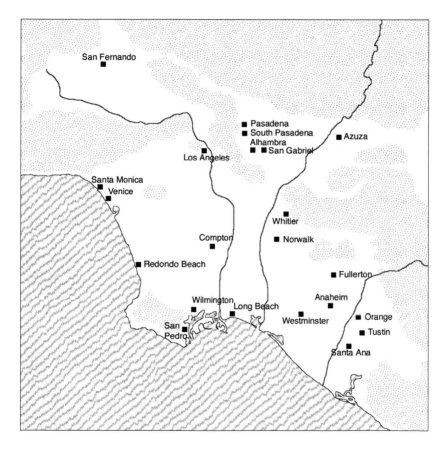

Fig. 42   Towns with a 1900 population of 500 or more.

ulation of five hundred or more had been established by indigenous peoples.

The placement of indigenous villages required a sophisticated knowledge of the local landscape. Place names reveal an intimate environmental appreciation as opposed to a picturesque sentimentality. Instead of referring to distant images (Hawaiian Gardens, Rustic Canyon, Hidden Hills), indigenous place names reflected immediate qualities. Cahuegna (Cahuenga) meant "place in the little hills," Kukamogna (Rancho Cucamonga) meant "sandy place," Topagna (Topanga) "place where the mountains run into the sea," Sukagna (Whittier) "place of wild bees," Suangna (San Pedro) "place of rushes," Kingkingna (San Pedro) "houses by the sea," Munikangna (San Pedro) "place of the small-large hill."[18]

Villages were commonly located on the high ground in the shelter of oak trees, on the open coastal plains, along the banks of rivers and at the seashore.[19] In his letters of 1852, Hugo Reid estimated the number of villages at sixty-seven.[20] While that number was edited down to forty-three, regional maps provide a range in between. Reid cited the largest village (Suangna) as containing from 500 to 1,500 huts.[21] Coastal villages were occupied continuously[22] and included: Chowingna (Malaga Cove

Fig. 43

Fig. 44

in Torrance)[23], Puvugna (on the back of Alamitos Bay)[24] and Saangna (near the mouth of the Ballona Creek in Playa Del Rey). [43] Portola's scouts reported a village inland from Santa Monica where another creek ran south (approximately at the site of Veteran's Hospital in Westwood) [44] near where there is a still existing natural spring.[25]

Gabrielino villages were more generously spaced then other California tribes. Unlike the Karok (who distributed their settlements along year-round flowing streams), the Nisenan (who distributed their villages near year-round streams or around edges of small lakes and valleys), or even their neighbors the Chumash (who grew in number closer to the coastline, clustering their large villages by the shore), the Gabrielino took advantage of a wide variety and combination of environmental features. Permanent indigenous settlements appear mainly near the intersection of two or more environmental zones.[26]

Although the Gabrielino as a whole were self-sufficient, individual triblets were less so. To subsist on a varied food source during times of abundance and scarcity, communication between triblets was essential. Intermarriage between tribal members from differing environmental zones (coastal, prairie, foothill) was greatly encouraged so as to maintain healthy relations between villages. And because of the importance of communication, villages were not only related to the natural environment, but also to a larger system of paths and trade routes. The indigenous path system led to natural resources, other villages and other tribal territories.

The largest resource was, of course, the ocean. Foothills provided abundant vegetation for harvesting and game for hunting. Rivers provided fresh water and fish. Tar deposits in mid-city were important for basketry and housing. Salt, crusted on rushes, was available from marshes. Fresh water was available not only from rivers, but from creeks and numerous natural underground springs such as Serra, Los Alamitos, Encino and Centinela. [45]

Equally as important, trails led to other villages and out to other tribal territories for the purposes of visitation, harvest, ceremony, marriage, ritual and trade. Trade, critical to indigenous subsistence required the design and maintenance of a road system that was not casual, but instead a sophisticated undertaking born of necessity. The result of that undertaking laid the groundwork for our city's freeways.

Archeological findings provide evidence supporting the importance of this path/settle-

Fig. 45

Fig. 46

ment relationship. A documented village by an important path lies near Rancho Los Encinos. [46] Aerial photographs taken prior to the widening of Ventura Boulevard show a circular mound near the old road and Rancho. In 1984-5 archaeolgical excavations prior to speculative construction revealed evidence of as much as 7,000 years of human inhabitation.[27] Tragically, a multi-story office complex and a subterranean parking garage now cover this site. [47]

A more entact village site lays just inside the Los Angeles County line. This shell mound by Pacific Coast Highway shows a similar path/settlement relationship. [48-50] It is speculated that this village, unlike Malaga Cove or Encino, was of relatively short duration, having contained artifacts dating from approximately 1,500 years ago until about 1800-1830. Although a Chumash village, archeological evidence indicates substantial trade with their southern neighbors.

From wilderness to inner-city, throughout Southern California, archeological evidence indicates peoples that were anything but sedentary. The regularity in which villages were found adjacent to major roads reveals that not only can Los Angeles' original inhabitants be credited with the placement of major population centers, but with the layout of the roads that

Fig. 47

Fig. 48

Fig. 49

Fig. 50

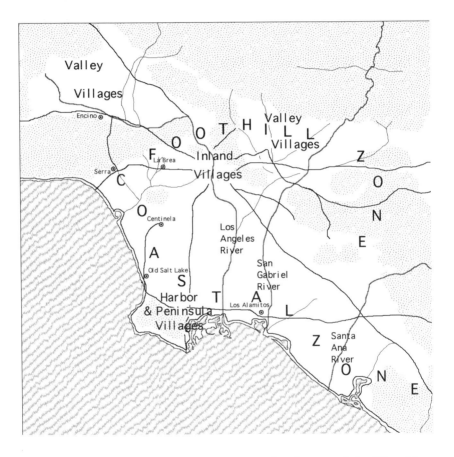

Settlement pattern & lines of communication model   Fig. 51

Fig. 52

Freeway) was an ancient interstate trade route. Another interstate route, this one leading east along the Puente and San Jose Hills was also to become a major freeway.[34] Indigenous guides showed Portola both the Cahuenga and Sepulveda passes through the Santa Monica Mountains. Portola was also guided through the Puente Hills, then along a route later to become the Pomona Freeway.

Other contemporary lines of communication were also of indigenous origin. A major intersection of indigenous trails was at Gaffey, Vermont, Anaheim and Palos Verdes Drive North.[35] Gaffey led south to numerous other villages. Anaheim Street is the old Anaheim-Wilmington Road which once led to several villages along the Santa Ana River. Palos Verdes North and Pacific Coast Highway led first to Engnovangna (Redondo Beach), to Saangna (Playa Del Rey) at the mouth of the Ballona Creek, then possibly on to other coastal villages. Train tracks and avenues trace the Old Salt Road which led out from Engnovagna to a native source of fresh water at Centinela Springs.[36]

Whittier Boulevard is a tracing of one branch of the Los Angeles-Whittier Road (itself a branch of the Camino Real which was in turn a tracing of indigenous trails). San Fernando

Fig. 53

Road, leading from Pasecgna to Yangna, became first a Mission Road, then a rail and trolley route, then a freeway (the 5 Golden State). Several other major freeways follow the paths of local rivers and creeks, and our very first freeway (the 110 Pasadena Freeway) follows the Arroyo Seco along which were numerous villages. In Ord's 1849 "Survey of the Los Angeles Plains and Vicinity," four trails lead out from the city, all of indigenous origin. From the first railroads to the Pacific Electric Cars to the modern freeway system, many of our local lines of communication were a tracing of the indigenous system of trade and migration routes.[37]

Although Spanish, Mexican and American societies mimicked the existing indigenous settlement pattern, they also obviously made massive change. The most significant structural change was the initial demographic shift—the sucking of population from outlying regions in the form of forced labor and the centralization of population and power inland. This resulted in the dominant role of the Pueblo (downtown) that lasted until the middle of the twentieth century.

Dismissing native cultures as primitive, the Spanish commandeered the villages of Pasecgna (San Fernando),[38] and Sibagna (San

Fig. 54

Fig. 55

Fig. 56

Gabriel)[39] [55-57], for forced labor in their missions, then later, the village of Yangna for their pueblo.[40] The area's native population before occupation was conservatively estimated at five thousand,[41] however by 1836 the first official census showed a population of 553.[42]

This ruthless pattern was not only present in Los Angeles County but throughout the state. Estimates of state wide aboriginal population before European contact range from 133,000 to 310,000. In the first one hundred years of Spanish, Mexican and American settlement, that number was reduced by 85% and thirty years later by 95%.[43]

The purpose of establishing the Pueblo was chiefly to supply the Spanish military. Los Angeles attached itself to Yangna and immediately utilized native labor. By the 1830s, disease and forced labor had decimated the village. Those still able to work were enslaved—paid with liquor, arrested for drunkenness, and then auctioned off to work as punishment. As common throughout California, native women were forced into prostitution. The village site had become the "Barbary Coast of the town"; it was purchased, then subsequently "abolished as a nuisance," its inhabitants expelled.[44] One historian places the village approximately beneath the old Bella Union Hotel, now Fletcher

Fig. 57

Bowron Square. [58-62]

Implicit in the establishment of the Pueblo and the centralization of the population was the subdivision of land through the use of a grid. The Pueblo followed the Spanish Law of the Indies[45] and established this pattern of development, setting the tone for the outlying towns. Rancho ownership was codified in 1836 when all claimants in the county were required to file a survey of their lands.[46] This indicated that although rancho population (dispersed throughout the territory) almost equaled that of the Pueblo, dependency on the center for authority, security and partial supply was still in place.

Ranchos reoccupied village sites. Subdivision laid a grid over the ranchos. Boomtowns, governed by the same general zoning codes as central Los Angeles, became miniature downtowns, each with their own main commercial street and characteristic orientation to natural amenities (for example, Santa Monica was oriented to the shore, La Puente to the mountains). The difference between the center and the satellites was size, scale and lines of communication.

By the time of the first census, the grid of the pueblo had expanded considerably. A survey was commissioned in 1849 and it shows a

Fig. 58

Fig. 59

Fig. 60

Fig. 61

Fig. 62

small off compass grid divided into two parts at the base of a set of hills to the west. Main Street forms the eastern border to the farmlands and empty plots beyond. By the time of the 1884 Stevenson Map, these two parts had unified and were branching out in all directions. This represented the city's first major boom. [63]

True, the Spanish commandeered native lands and enslaved indigenous peoples. The Mexicans continued this practice and further divided large parcels, resulting in overgrazing and the destruction of the ecosystem. But it took the Americans to turn a small town into a profit-making machine.

The factors that led to the boom of the 1880s included the Santa Fe Railroad choosing Los Angeles as its Pacific terminus and real estate investor sponsered promotional campaigns that portrayed outlying regions as near paradises. Health seekers and tourists came from the east and purchased land in all areas of the county. The Stevenson Map shows a rapidly expanding downtown, but the Lankershim Ranch Land and Water Company map of 1888 shows dozens of miniature downtowns, following the same codes, most all sprouting from rancho settlements which had in turn sprouted from indigenous villages. Both the Lankershim Ranch Land and Water Company map of 1888

Fig. 63

and the Stool and Thayer Sectional and Road map of 1900 show a Southern California with a single larger central city, and, outlying smaller developments that (with few exceptions) were stops along railroad routes (leading out from downtown) which were in turn indigenous routes.[47]

Not only did the city's organization grow from both indigenous and European roots, but the "give and take" pattern of the two systems is manifested consistently throughout Los Angeles' history. Once the population center had relocated, the demographic relationship between center and satellites remained surprisingly stable (half in the city and half in the other parts of the county) for the next one hundred-fifty years.

By 1890, the city population was 50,393, county population 101,454 and by 1900, the city population was 102,479, county population 170,298. By the 1920s, centralized growth had extended out to places such as Echo Park, Vernon and Alhambra, while outlying towns now included places such as Burbank, Hollywood and Culver City. By the late 1930s, downtown's climax was subsiding and the center would continue to wind down through the following decade. By then, the first freeway had traced the riverbed route of the Arroyo Seco into Pasadena and the emboldening of the path system had begun. By 1950, the Hollywood Freeway (tracing the Camino Real), the San Bernardino Freeway (tracing a Mission Road later to be called Old San Bernardino Road) and the Santa Ana Freeway (also tracing the Camino Real) had all begun construction. [64-66] The population of the city fell to less than that of county for the first time since the nineteenth century. By 1960, the city's population had been reduced to two-fifths of the county's.[48] Currently it remains at this same level but the city's boundaries include places as distant as the San Fernando Valley to the north, San Pedro to the south, Venice to the west and Eagle Rock to the east so that even that two-fifths statistic has melted into its counter-statistic. Once the dominant center of a region, many now argue that downtown is but another piece of many pieces that make up the puzzle of our city.

A puzzle. A puzzle that has become not only difficult to grasp but difficult to comprehend as well. Once a low-impact, sustainable system, our city grew, not gradually, but explosively. It is now organized not in one way, not in two ways, but in two ways that have melded together. Its center is no longer dominant, nor is it just another outlying town. Because of the violence of our transitions, our constant motion, our accelerated pace, our ignorance of our own nature, our blind eye to the past and our sacrifice of order for organization, Los Angeles has indeed become bleak—bleak, caught in limbo and without footing. Once we were scattered dots, circles and wiggly lines. Now the dots are bunched in crowds, the circles have become squares and the wiggly lines do everything possible to appear straight.

Yet when we look at the duration of basin settlement, whether over distant space or distant time, we find a less complex relationship. The organizations of grids and lines fade, and we see that our city, despite its technological prowess, cannot escape the power of nature. Like the leaves falling upon the banks of Harbor Lake, our city is part of a cycle. Inescapably, it will soon be ruins, buried, and we, just as were the peoples before us, forgotten.

For the time being, though, Los Angeles, like the crashing surf in Torrance, is mighty, violent and relentless. Like the cactus on the trellis in San Gabriel, two systems have become one. Like the plaster statue on Mission Road, gigantic and powerful, but empty, without will, without awareness. Like the water fountain in Inglewood, trickling away its remaining resources, draining its own life. And like the bird and the cat in Wilmington, passed on, transforming, becoming something else, as we ants hurriedly follow in lines from the eye of the animal to our home in the anthill.

***

1Maps represent built-up areas. Michael W. Donley, *Atlas of California* (Culver City: Pacific Book Center, 1979).

2The Law of the Indies and its influence on the Pueblo are most clearly described in John W. Reps, *Town Planning in Frontier America* (Princeton: Princeton University Press, 1969), pp. 64-68.

3With its clear diagrams, maps and powerful argument, Reyner Banham, *Los Angeles: The Architecture of Four Ecologies (*New York: Penguin Books, 1971) led the way with this view which is still predominant. This book was published immediately after the razing of Bunker Hill and prior to the investment of billions downtown.

4*Cities in Our Future-Growth & Form, Environmental Health and Social Equity* (Covelo, California: Island Press, 1997).

5David Hornbeck, *California Patterns: A Geographical and Historical Atlas* (Palo Alto: Mayfield Publishing, 1983), pp. 32-33. Locations on the Indigenous Villages map from figure nine is mainly from "Territories of the Gabrielino and Adjoining Tribes" (mainly after Johnston (1962: map)).

6The locations are mainly according to Agusta Fink, *Palos Verdes Peninsula-Time and Terraced Land* (Santa Cruz: West Tanger Press, 1987), pg. 24. Other sources include: "Territories of the Gabrielino and Adjoining Tribes" (mainly after Johnston (1962: map)), "The

Gabrielino Indians at the Time of the Portola Expedition" (Southwest Museum, 1962), Dr. Lois J. Weinman, *Los Angeles-Long Beach Harbor Areas-Cultural Resource Survey* (Los Angeles: U.S. Army Engineer District, 1978).

7William McCawley, *The First Angelinos-The Gabrielino Indians of Los Angeles* (Banning: Malki Museum Press/Ballena Press, 1996), pp. 66-69.

8Thomas Brothers Maps (Irvine, California, 1987). The 1987 *Thomas Guide* indicates a park named "Suangna Village Park." This park is no longer indicated on current guides. There are also two historic plaques located miles apart that indicate the location of Suangna. See Judson A. Grenier, *A Guide to Historic Places in Los Angeles County* (Dubuque: Kendall/Hunt Publishing Company, 1978).

9Judson A. Grenier, *A Guide to Historic Places in Los Angeles County* (Dubuque: Kendall/Hunt Publishing Company, 1978), Henry P. Silka, *San Pedro-A Pictorial History* (San Pedro: San Pedro Bay Historical Society, 1984), and Agusta Fink, *Palos Verdes Peninsula: Time and Terraced Land* (Santa Cruz: Western Tanger Press, 1987) all place Suangna on the north side of the hill overlooking Harbor Lake specifically on land that is now on the grounds of the oil refinery. Dr. Lois J. Weinman, *Los Angeles-Long Beach Harbor Areas-Cultural Resource Survey* (Los Angeles: U.S. Army Engineer District, 1978) places Mausuangna approximately at this site with Suangna further east. W.W. Robinson, *San Pedro and Wilmington-A Calendar of Events in the Making of Two Cities and the Los Angeles Harbor* (Los Angeles: Title Guarantee and Trust Company, 1942) places Suangna further south. William

Fig. 64

McCawley, *The First Angelinos-The Gabrielino Indians of Los Angeles* (Banning: Malki Museum Press/Ballena Press, 1996) offers considerable additional locational information.

10Judson A. Grenier, *A Guide to Historic Places in Los Angeles County* (Dubuque: Kendall/Hunt Publishing Company, 1978), pg 195. Also see, W.W. Robinson, *Ranchos Become Cities* (Pasadena: San Pasqual Press, 1939).

11According to Henry P. Silka, *San Pedro-A Pictorial History* (San Pedro: San Pedro Bay Historical Society, 1984), p. 12-13, portions of this extensive village were still inhabited as late as the 1850s. Also see William McCawley, *The First Angelinos-The Gabrielino Indians of Los Angeles* (Banning: Malki Museum Press/Ballena Press, 1996).

12The change of name of local lakes from Spanish to English reflected racial attitudes of the period. For example, the name "La Laguna" was changed to "Nigger Slough". See George W. Kirkman, 1937, "Kirkman-Harriman Pictorial and Historic Map of Los Angeles County" (as of 1860).

13Judson A. Grenier, *A Guide to Historic Places in Los Angeles County* (Dubuque: Kendall/Hunt Publishing Company, 1978), pg 175.

14David Gebhard and Robert Winter, *Los Angeles-An Architectural Guide* (Salt Lake City: Gibbs-Smith Publisher, 1994), pg. 61

15"The Gabrielino Indians at the Time of the Portola Expedition" (Southwest Museum, 1962) marks this village as Suvangna (Sehat). Alfred L. Kroeber, *Handbook of the Indians of California* (Berkeley: California Book Company, Ltd., 1925) marks it as Sehat. George W.

Kirkman, 1937, "Kirkman-Harriman Pictorial and Historic Map of Los Angeles County" (as of 1860) also indicates a village just north of Whittier. Also see W.W. Robinson, *Ranchos Become Cities* (Pasadena: San Pasqual Press, 1939), pg. 63.

16W. W. Robinson, *Ranchos Become Cities* (Pasadena: San Pasqual Press, 1939), pg. 64.

17David Gebhard and Robert Winter, *Los Angeles-An Architectural Guide* (Salt Lake City: Gibbs-Smith Publisher, 1994), pg. 306.

18Agusta Fink, *Palos Verdes Peninsula: Time and Terraced Land* (Santa Cruz: Western Tanger Press, 1987). Also, W.W. Robinson, *Ranchos Become Cities* (Pasadena: San Pasqual Press, 1939).

19Bruce W. Miller, *The Gabrielino* (Los Osos: Sand River Press, 1991), pg. 2.

20Hugo Reid, edited by Robert F. Heizer, *The Indians of Los Angeles County-Hugo Reid's Letters of 1852* (Highland Park, Southwest Museum, 1962).

21Maps of indigenous settlements show a cluster of villages in the harbor. With its abundandant food supply and relationship with the Channel Islands, it is possible that the harbor area was of special importance. "The Gabrielino Indians at the Time of the Portola Expedition" (Los Angeles: Southwest Museum, 1962), shows nine villages in this area, George W. Kirkman, 1937, "Kikman-Harriman Pictorial and Historic Map of Los Angeles County" (as of 1860), shows four. Agusta Fink, *Palos Verdes Peninsula: Time and Terraced Land* (Santa Cruz: Western Tanger Press, 1987), pg. 24, provided several more locations including the village of Tsavingna as being located near the site of the original town of San Pedro. Also indicated are possible addition

Fig. 65

nameless village locations. Dr. Lois J. Weinman, *Los Angeles-Long Beach Harbor Areas-Cultural Resource Survey* (Los Angeles: U.S. Army Engineer District, 1978), pg. 15, provides a map of nine villages. Also see Hugo Reid, edited by Robert F. Heizer, *The Indians of Los Angeles County-Hugo Reid's Letters of 1852* (Highland Park, Southwest Museum, 1962).

22Sarah R. Lombard, *Rancho Tujunga-A History of Sunland/Tujunga, California* (Burbank, Bridge Publishing, 1990), pg 2.

23While several maps indicate this village as being further inland, Edwin Francis Walker, *Five Prehistoric Archaeological Sites in Los Angeles County California* (Los Angeles: Southwest Museum, 1952), describes this place as "The site of a large and flourishing village of Chowingna."

24This village is also confirmed by at least four sources. W. W. Robinson, *Ranchos Become Cities* (Pasadena: San Pasqual Press, 1939), pg. 50, indicates the location as being at the back of the Alamitos Bay (Los Alamitos).

25The location by Ballona Creek is labeled in Alfred L. Kroeber, *Handbook of the Indians of California* (Berkeley: California Book Company, Ltd., 1925). It is indicated on George W. Kirkman, 1937, "Kirkman-Harriman Pictorial and Historic Map of Los Angeles County" (as of 1860). It is shown bordered by archaeological sites on "The Gabrielino Indians at the Time of the Portola Expedition" (Los Angeles: Southwest Museum, 1962). It is also described in W. W. Robinson, *Ranchos Become Cities* (Pasadena, San Pasqual Press, 1939), pg. 130. The spring located on the campus of University High School is indicated on George W. Kirkman, 1937, "Kikman-Harriman Pictorial and

Historic Map of Los Angeles County" (as of 1860), and described in W.W. Robinson, *Ranchos Become Cities* (Pasadena, San Pasqual Press, 1939), pp. 144-5. This last location is also described in Judson A. Grenier, *A Guide to Historic Places in Los Angeles County* (Dubuque: Kendall/Hunt Publishing Company, 1978), pp. 116.

26William McCawley, *The First Angelinos-The Gabrielino Indians of Los Angeles* (Banning: Malki Museum Press/Ballena Press, 1996), pg. 26. For Aboriginal Subsistence Patterns, see David Hornbeck, *California Patterns: A Geographical and Historical Atlas* (Palo Alto: Mayfield Publishing, 1983), pg. 36.

27William McCawley, *The First Angelinos-The Gabrielino Indians of Los Angeles* (Banning: Malki Museum Press/Ballena Press, 1996). The name and location of more sensitive and still entact sites were excluded in the essay and footnotes. One source was also excluded. Specific locations of harbor villages were also made more general.

28W.W. Robinson, *Ranchos Become Cities* (Pasadena: San Pasqual Press, 1939), pg. 156. Also see W.W. Robinson, *Los Angeles from the days of the Pueblo* (Menlo Park: Calif. Historical Society, 1959), pg. 22. Also see W.W. Robinson, *History of the Miracle Mile* (Los Angeles: Columbia Savings and Loan Association, 1965).

29Crespi reported a "village of heathen Indians out gathering their seeds." Fernando Boneu, *Gaspar de Portolá-Explorer and Founder of California* (Lerida, Instituto de Estudios Ilerdenses, 1983), pg. 175.

30Fernando Boneu, *Gaspar de Portolá-Explorer and Founder of California* (Lerida, Instituto de Estudios

Ilerdenses, 1983), pp. 288-292.

31Evidence seems especially strong for this ancient Los Angeles County communication system as villages subsisted more on fish and locally harvested acorn and other crops rather than having followed the migration of large mammals. The routes to and from the natural resources of salt, tar, fresh spring water, marshes and estuaries correspond with contemporary lines of communciation. See James T. Davis, *Trade Routes and Economic Exchange Among the Indians of California* (Ramona: Ballena Press, 1974), pg. 4. For corroborating information, see Sarah R. Lombard, *Rancho Tujunga-A History of Sunland/Tujunga, California* (Burbank, Bridge Publishing, 1990), pg 2.

32George W. Kirkman, 1937, "Kirkman-Harriman Pictorial and Historic Map of Los Angeles County" (as of 1860).

33John D. Weaver, *El Pueblo Grande-Los Angeles From the Brush Huts of the Yangna to the Skyscrapers of the Modern Megalopolis* (Private Printer: Los Angeles, 1973).

34David Hornbeck, *California Patterns: A Geographical and Historical Atlas* (Palo Alto: Mayfield Publishing, 1983), pg. 32.

35Henry P. Silka, *San Pedro-A Pictorial History* (San Pedro: San Pedro Bay Historical Society, 1984), pp. 12-13.

36George W. Kirkman, 1937, "Kirkman-Harriman Pictorial and Historic Map of Los Angeles County" (as of 1860).

37David Hornbeck, *California Patterns: A Geographical and Historical Atlas* (Palo Alto: Mayfield Publishing, 1983), pg. 32. George W. Kirkman, 1937,

"Kirkman-Harriman Pictorial and Historic Map of Los Angeles County" (as of 1860). Lt. E.O.C. Ord, "Topographical Sketch of the Los Angeles Plains and Vicinity," August, 1849. See also James T. Davis, *Trade Routes and Economic Exchange Among the Indians of California* (Ramona: Ballena Press, 1974), pg. 4. Even popular fiction writer Louis Lamour discusses the ancient indigenous trails in his novel, *The Californios*.

38Hugo Reid calls this village Pasecgna. It also appears on the following: George W. Kirkman, 1937, "Kirkman-Harriman Pictorial and Historic Map of Los Angeles County" (as of 1860), Alfred L. Kroeber, *Handbook of the Indians of California* (Berkeley: California Book Company, Ltd., 1925). "The Gabrielino Indians at the Time of the Portola Expedition" (Los Angeles: Southwest Museum, 1962). An account by Father De Santa Maria reads, "In this place we came to a rancheria near the dwelling of said Reyes—with enough Indians." This confirms to some degree that missionaries were not so interested in conversion as in exploitation. A requirement for siting of the new mission was proximity to a source of labor.

39This location is indicated by at least seven sources. It is on George W. Kirkman, 1937, "Kirkman-Harriman Pictorial and Historic Map of Los Angeles County" (as of 1860). Alfred L. Kroeber, *Handbook of the Indians of California* (Berkeley: California Book Company, Ltd., 1925), "The Gabrielino Indians at the Time of the Portola Expedition", (Los Angeles: Southwest Museum, 1962), and is listed by Reid and Robinson. Heizer adds an additional two sources.

40Fernando Boneu, *Gaspar de Portolá-Explorer and*

Fig. 66

Founder of California (Lerida, Instituto de Estudios Ilerdenses, 1983) reports the presence of the Portola expedition at this village. Also see George W. Kirkman, 1937, "Kirkman-Harriman Pictorial and Historic Map of Los Angeles County" (as of 1860); Alfred L. Kroeber, *Handbook of the Indians of California* (Berkeley: California Book Company, Ltd., 1925); and "The Gabrielino Indians at the Time of the Portola Expedition" (Los Angeles: Southwest Museum, 1962). W.W. Robinson, *Los Angeles From the Days of the Pueblo* (Menlo Park: California Historical Society, 1959), pg. 12, indicates the probable location near Main Street and the 101 Freeway.

41This estimate by Kroeber seems conservative given the number of villages and number of huts estimated by Reid.

42This was the number of "domesticated Indians." Disease, forced labor, torture and execution had killed the majority of the indigenous peoples.

43David Hornbeck, *California Patterns* (Palo Alto: Mayfield Publishing, 1983), pp. 34-35.

44 According to Robert Mayer, *Los Angeles: a chronological and documentary history, 1542-1976* (Dobbs Ferry, New York: Oceana Publication, Inc. 1978), "John Groningen purchased the Indian Village Yangna from the city and expelled the remaining Indians. The place had become the Barbary Coast of the town and was abolished as a nuisance." This description along with accounts of pueblo and rancho forced labor through use of alcohol addiction paint a sad picture for the remaining indigenous peoples. The site according to W.W. Robinson, *Los Angeles From the Days of the Pueblo* (Menlo Park: California Historical Society, 1959), pg.

12, is possibly the former location of the Los Angeles Star and Bella Union Hotel, now called Fletcher Bowron Square. If this is so, a good portion of the village was most likely unearthed during construction of the 101 Hollywood Freeway.

45John W. Reps, *Town Planning in Frontier America* (Princeton: Princeton University Press, 1969), pg. 64.

46Mayer, Robert, *Los Angeles: a chronological and documentary history, 1542-1976* (Dobbs Ferry, New York: Oceana Publication, Inc. 1978).

47"Lankershim Ranch Land and Water Company Map" (Los Angeles, 1988). Also, H.J. Stevenson, U.S. Department Surveyor, "Map of the City of Los Angeles, 1884."

48Robert Mayer, *Los Angeles: a chronological and documentary history, 1542-1976* (Dobbs Ferry, New York: Oceana Publication, Inc. 1978).

Fig. 1

Asparagus Patch

The bright Southern California sun, throughout summer, spring and fall, reflects sharply off the glass surfaces of Los Angeles' new skyline. In winter, however, a gray fog can give the towers an eerie appearance. [1] Wind and drizzle blow through empty plazas, around abstract steel sculptures, along lines of planter bushes, and over beds of carefully tended flowers.

Only thirty years ago, these same gusts could be seen billowing the curtains of antique houses, clapboard apartments and brick hotels. Bunker Hill used to be a quaint old-fashioned residential neighborhood. Steps ran up steep inclines, benches faced city views, narrow alleys ran behind rows of buildings, streetcars rumbled through tunnels underneath and wind breaks of mature trees swayed up top. It was a place that had developed slowly, maturing gracefully over time. [2]

Prior to the "redevelopment" of the hill, writer Kevin Lynch included it in his 1960 urban study *The Image of the City*. It may seem surprising to today's reader that Los Angeles was selected not for its smog, diverse population, lines of freeways, or notoriety for violence, but instead for its "utterly different scale and central grid iron plan."[1]

"As the core of a metropolis, central Los Angeles is heavily charged with meaning and activity, with large and presumably distinctive buildings, and with a basic pattern: its almost regular grid of streets."[2]

Lynch's map of visual form indicates Pershing Square as a central node "sitting in the crook" of Seventh Street and Broadway. The Bunker Hill "district" was described in the study[3] as having a "relatively weak" urban image.[4] Some would argue that this evaluation applies more accurately today, but why was Bunker Hill seen in that light then?

The early sixties was a time when belief in "progress" was predominant. The U.S. had entered the space age. Televisions and appliances were in most homes. Cartoons like *The Jetsons* featured families living in floating houses and running errands in flying bubble cars while programs such as *The Addams Family* and

Fig. 2

The Munsters presented antique homes as dwellings for misfits [3]. James Bond's gadgets gave him power and sex appeal while a common California Gothic mansion, in the movie *Psycho*, was a venue for mental illness and murder. Buckminster Fuller's Geodesic Dome was heroically inventive while a common brick building, the Texas Schoolbook Depository, was embedded in the national mind as a hideout nest for treachery. Even though through the early part of the century, Victorian Houses set the scene for serious drama, by the fifties, every Mr. Chicken was running bug-eyed through the halls bumping into suits of armor and fainting at the sight of a player organ.

This is not to say that Bunker Hill did not have its own particular character. Its topography kept it apart—never quite within downtown. Bunker Hill houses remained while the wood and adobe residences on Broadway gave way, first to brick stores, then later to steel and concrete offices. Still residential in the 1860s, by the late 1880s, Broadway and Spring were for working and shopping, the "Hill" was to go home to. And what connected those buggy-congested corridors of commerce to the turreted Queen Annes and English primrose gardens above? Steep roads, several sets of steps, and a famous little trolley. [4]

Fig. 3

That Angels Flight became an object of popular imagination is not surprising. It represented the simple solution to an essential local dilemma. How to connect our "strictly business" central business district to our humble hilltop homes? Little did the riders of that funky franchise funicular suspect that their grandchildren would bring new meaning to the word commute.

During the life of Angels Flight, the city and its modes of transportation changed frequently. Tunnels were blasted, horses were replaced by cable cars, cable cars by the Pacific Electric Cars, and the railways by automobiles, freeways and traffic.[5]

From the early 1930s to the late 1940s, the density of Bunker Hill rose to more than three persons per acre as a demographic shift took place.[6] Tenements housed the newcomers, low rents attracting people of all ages and races. Views of the city, mature trees along sidewalks, vigorous gardens and less traffic all created a bucolic neighborly presence.

By the 1950s, having recognized the value of the land, the Community Redevelopment Agency (CRA), Housing Authority and City Council had begun obtaining Bunker Hill property through eminent domain. By the 1960s, they had started razing

Fig. 4

buildings and clearing away old houses.[7] The final week of discounted rides was an ironically joyous one for Angels Flight. The neglected little train suddenly received abundant attention as lines of parents and children waited patiently to take their souvenir last ride. Then in the dark of night, after seven decades of service, Angels Flight was dismantled and carted away. [5]

After a thirty-year absence, the train is back—restored in 1996 to once again connect the upper and lower levels of downtown. During its absence though much has changed. And much like the refurbished cable cars Olivet and Sinai, questions about the downtown dilemma travel back and forth. Is downtown now a center or just another district? How does its past relate to its present and future? What remains of downtown's old structure? What should be preserved and what replaced? In short, what is downtown Los Angeles? To find out, let's stroll down Seventh to Broadway, double back to Pershing Square, then take the famous Angels Flight up to the new Bunker Hill.

We begin on Seventh and Hope. To the east is the abandoned J.W. Robinson's Department Store; to the west, Macy's Plaza.[8] While the front face of the "plaza" sports a grand escalator entrance, its south side resem-

Fig. 5

bles a fortress. [6] The base of this brick mass is without openings as if to resist attack. The intermediate section has slotted windows, but the upper portion (unlike medieval castles which tended to celebrate the sky with turrets, pinnacles and spires) is blank, returning instead to the hostility begun on the sidewalk.

Ironically, the more accessible J.W. Robinson Company Building was, in its day, equally exclusive. [7] Near opposite to Macy's in scale and fenestration pattern, Robinson's, ninety-five years ago, also rejected downtown throngs. Departing from the congestion of Broadway, it was one of the first stores in the nation to provide basement parking. Moving west on Seventh to what was then the edge of downtown, it positioned itself strategically in relation to upscale shoppers. In so doing, Robinson's strengthened Seventh Street to the point that it could serve as a second commercial corridor.[9] This created the downtown cross-axis that exists to this day. [8]

One block east on Seventh, we find the recently closed doors of Clifton's Silver Spoon Cafeteria. Its sister restaurant, Brookdale on Broadway, remains open and represents the last downtown remnant of the dreams of Clifford Clinton who financed many a fantastic, folksy and melodious ambiance for eating. These

Fig. 6

Fig. 7

Fig. 8

days, at Brookdale, coffee klatsches communicate in sign language on the ground floor while the children of Central American families run to get their free balloon upstairs. [9] Sixty years ago, during the Depression, instead of receiving a free prize, customers who did not have enough money were allowed to pay what they could afford.

Clinton seemed to have enjoyed gift giving and likewise abhorred corruption. So much so that just two years after Clifton's Brookdale opened in 1935, he promoted a grand jury investigation of no less than the LAPD and Mayor Frank Shaw. A few month's later, Clinton's home was bombed and in January of 1938 a witness against the Mayor was nearly killed when he triggered another explosive device wired to his car's ignition. Two officers and the chief of the Police Intelligence Bureau were convicted for the bombing and the Mayor was removed from office in a special recall election.[10] Clinton, after this reforming crusade, returned to his former business and to this day, the Brookdale Cafeteria on Broadway remains near intact. A stuffed moose (formerly a buck), an opaque sliver of moon, a polished redwood tree trunk and an indoor waterfall are among the interior splendors for the young and young at heart. And as if all that excitement weren't

Fig. 9

Fig. 10

enough, it seems now as though Clinton's decorative style may have caught on. Just a few blocks to the north in the lobby of the Ronald Reagan State Building, the arrangement of murals, trees, fountains and animal statues corresponds faithfully to its predecessor. Why is it though that the spirit of public generosity cannot seem to extend itself past the ground floor? [10]

As we proceed to the famous intersection of Seventh and Broadway, we are but a stone's throw from several of the other department stores that shaped downtown. The Bullock's Building still sits on the northwest corner, one block south on Eighth remains the May Company Building (formerly Hamburger's) and up ahead is the Broadway State Building (formerly the original Broadway Department Store).

Looking around at the results of this enterprise, we detect a distinct character to this collection of early twentieth century buildings. [11] The height limit, signage and surface textures are twentieth century products, but the wide sidewalks and grid iron layout came before. The quarter-compass northwest-southeast direction of Broadway was mandated in the late 1700s.[11] The short regular blocks appear on a Nineteenth century survey when the street was called Calle de Eternidad, then Buena Vista, then Fortin and as late as 1894, Fort Street.[12] At that time, the street was widened, paved and installed with sewers. It was, by then, a richly textured Yankee commercial corridor; cable cars ran past blocks of ornate facades while horses pulled buggies in between stone curbs. [12-13]

The facades changed in the early twentieth century but characteristically stayed just as ornate. Several buildings remain from this period including the Orpheum-1911,[13] Clune's Broadway Theater-1910,[14] and the Pantages Theater-1911.[15] These were nickelodeon and vaudeville theaters that added marquees and removed their sidewalk sandwich-board posters when later converted into movie theaters.

During the decade of the 1920s, the city's population grew from 576,677 to 1,238,048, taking it from the tenth largest city in the U.S. to the fifth. This was probably Broadway's most prosperous decade, and even though liquor was prohibited, the street was a center of night life. Most of the buildings we see today (Reed Jewelers-1929, the Arcade Building-1922-23, Schauber's Cafeteria-1927, Tower Theater-1925-26, State Theater-1921, the Chapman Building-1923, Eastern Columbia Building-1929, Texaco/United Artists Building-1927,

Fig. 11

Fig. 12

Globe Theater-1921, Ninth and Broadway Building-1929, and the Women's Athletic Club-1924)[16] were all constructed then during the street's second major expansion.

During that boom, Los Angeles elites tried to out do each other by importing designers and craftsmen. Five and dime shoppers, soda fountain sippers and movie premiere gawkers would look up at lavish facades on newly built office blocks, (segregated) movie palaces[17] and upscale department stores.

This is when the creative vitality of the street reached its peak; when its outlandish character blossomed. High hopes for twentieth century art and industry mixed with an adolescent exoticism and a somewhat nearsighted respect for the majesty of local landscape. When the economic egg timer rang and construction came to a dead halt in the mid-1930s, what had been turned out might be best decribed as half-baked.

Facade treatments included addorsed Greco cameramen and models seated atop opposing sides of Baroque broken pediments (Tower Theater) [14], bisonhead corbels and concrete bucranes with bronze longhorns (Million Dollar Theater) [15-16], and above the Palace marquee, a series of terra-cotta bas-relief dance hall minstrels   There is a sweeping

Fig. 14

Fig. 15

Fig. 16

Spanish Renaissance cathedral arch, a mint green tile clock tower and a Churrigueresque coquillage accolade above a bald-headed eagle crown. There are cupid cornerpieces, Gothic devil's head brackets, lion medallions and beaded Greek urns galore. This was a reckless screaming wild ride of architectural expression. A populist thumbing of the nose at tradition, sticking out of the tongue at establishment, and bent-over full-mooning at the doctrines of modernity. [17-23]

By 1940, the city's population had increased to 1,504,277.[18] In early 1942, Broadway was blacked out (along with the rest of the city) in (paranoid) fear of attack from Japanese airplanes. Japanese-owned businesses had "Closing Out" sales, and by March, the first contingent of Japanese Angelenos (immigrants and American-born alike) were bused to the plank and tar paper barracks of Manzanar Relocation Camp.[19] In 1943, a race riot reached its peak as stationed sailors, soldiers, marines and others converged on downtown—halting streetcars, breaking into theaters and dragging local *pachucos* out into the street where they beat them and stripped them of their zoot suits. Police responded by arresting the Zoot-Suiters.[20]

In 1945, Broadway was again mobbed as

Fig. 17

Fig. 18

Fig. 19

Fig. 20

sirens signaled the end of the war, and later, there was an Armistice Parade. In 1948, the CRA was established and in 1952, the Hollywood Freeway cut through above Temple Street.[21] Although an established center of commerce and entertainment, Broadway was about to experience drastic change.

Given the smoggy start, it's a wonder Broadway saw its way out of the 1950s. On October 13, 1954, visibility was so poor city-wide that the airport was closed and ships were unable to enter the harbor. The population was now almost two million and freeways were sprouting everywhere. At that time, a new law created the Metropolitan Transportation Authority (MTA) and transferred contol of rapid transit (with Broadway as its central core) away from local authority.[22]

In 1960, JFK accepted the democratic nomination at the newly constructed Sports Arena. Downtown, his speech on the corner of Sixth and Broadway drew huge crowds. On March 31, 1963, the last streetcar retired from service, yet as buses retraced the same routes, Broadway remained the transportation hub. The following month, the Bunker Hill Urban Renewal Program was established.

Two years later and one hundred blocks due south, disturbances in the Watts district left

Fig. 21

Fig. 22

thirty-four dead, over one thousand injured, nearly four thousand arrested and two hundred buildings damaged.[23] This event and the succeeding disturbances six months later foreshadowed Broadway's experience of the early '90s.

Broadway rumbled into the next decade with the 1971 Sylmar earthquake leaving thirty-five dead and over $1 billion in damages citywide. By this time, the face of Broadway had changed to serve the city's vast Latino population as its predominate clientele. Although buildings were still well-maintained on the ground level, billboards proliferated, rooftop signs were turned off, and (by agreement with the city) upper floors were abandoned. While small businesses received little if any funding, the lack of "development" had its positive side as Broadway was able to retain its heritage of historic buildings.

Unfortunately, as uneven allocation of funds continued unabated throughout the '80s and major stores (Bullocks, Broadway, Mullen and Bluett, Grodens, Harris and Frank, Bonds Clothing and Silverwoods) all packed up and left, the stage was set for Broadway's most recent and perhaps most rigorous test.

On the night of April 29, 1992, soon after the not guilty verdicts in the trial of police officers who beat motorist Rodney King were

Fig. 23

announced, groups of outraged protesters outside of Parker Center broke away and began turning over police cars, setting fires and breaking into stores. Police, patrolled Grand in an armored personnel carrier and formed lines at East First and Los Angeles Streets, and, East Second and San Pedro Streets occupying the civic center and the high-investment properties of Bunker Hill (offices and hotels) and Little Tokyo (shopping malls and the New Otani Hotel), but leaving the more popularly-priced commercial corridor of Broadway open. Marching down the street, emerging from stores with merchandise in hand, shaking guard gates off of entrances, setting fires, that night, people released their anger and outrage on a place many were familiar with from shopping on during the day.

A few store owners rushed to protect their property while most waited out the four days before returning and salvaging what they could. Months later, while other areas of the city were still recovering, Broadway had swept up, and for the most part, gotten back on its feet.[24]

But just how sturdy is this Los Angeles landmark path? With layers of incomplete redevelopment plans piling up, developers, corporations, building owners and governmental agencies vying for control of the "historic core," and

Fig. 24

movie location crews increasingly treating it as their personal stage set, the future is uncertain for Los Angeles' most grand shopping corridor. [24]

As we consider these questions, let us detour briefly to what Kevin Lynch called the "node" of the city—Los Angeles' official chalk-board—Pershing Square. Every few decades, the park is wiped clean and given an entirely new design. It has had eight names, and only ten years ago, received its sixth makeover.[25] [25-27]

In 1986-7, an international Pershing Square design competition was held, five finalists were selected and an entry entitled the "Magic Carpet" was awarded first place. Shortly thereater, the winning design team[26] was paid an undisclosed amount by local developers MacGuire Thomas Partners. They, in turn, hired Mexican architect Ricardo Legorreta whose design of a yellow LAPD substation, a purple Styrofoam recorded music tower, a Luis Barragán[27] fountain and a collection of beige and pink five-foot diameter stucco spheres you see today.[28] The tropical trees, crowded lanes, lines of benches and speaker's corners are long gone, as will be this design in another ten or fifteen years. [28-32]

From here, we can spot, two blocks up

Fig. 25

Fig. 26

136

Fig. 27

Fig. 28

Fig. 29

Fig. 29

Fig. 30

Hill Street, the lower portal of Angels Flight. It was recently reinstalled to connect the state and federally subsidized Grand Central Square Project to the high rise towers above. The amount spent on Grand Central Square, so far, is roughly $55 million dollars and as we cross the street, we can multiply double that by every rail cross tie and still not approach the amount spent (through a handy accounting device called "tax incrementation") on the new Bunker Hill.

In its new context, the function of the train has changed. Before, a link between a residential district and its goods and services, now it is more of a tourist and lunch hour attraction. The upper portal, meticulously painted in its original orange and black, was once an attention-grabbing miniature fantasy object. In its new surroundings, it almost seems somber.

Aside from that ornamental wood arch, nothing from the old Bunker Hill is left. Not a gingerbread house, a buckled sidewalk, a tilting telephone pole, a meandering vine, an overgrown thicket, a rusting fire escape, a cactus garden or a cracked curb. As if a redevelopment bomb had been dropped, the neighborhood along with its residents, are all gone, vanished. [33]

Now the buildings (in what Charles Moore called the L.A. Asparagus Patch)[29] rise

Fig. 31

Fig. 32

Fig. 33

Fig. 34

Fig. 35

as high as their vacancy rates, each shouting for attention. "I'm an elegant dark tower," and "I'm a triangular pure form," and "I'm a post-modern masterpiece," and "I'm neo-classic," and "I'm deconstructivist." There are benches, but they are on private property. There are grand glass lobbies but entrance is selective. Public art and semi-private space are put out on display like consolation prizes at the county fair. Tourists refer to maps, lost in a limbo Land of Fragments, a redevelopment Outer Limits, an urban renewal Twilight Zone, a corporate Never-Never Land. [34-44]

But wasn't the hill a decaying neighborhood? Wasn't it a transient-filled slum, a skid-row shanty, a low-class welfare ghetto? What about the vice-infested bars and seedy flop houses we've read about in detective novels?

Although some authors used the hill as a setting for crime and decay, others such as Leo Politi presented more favorable descriptions. On film, pre-demolition Bunker Hill was perhaps best captured in a 1961 short documentary entitled *The Exiles* which followed the lives of a group of Navajo young people.[30] They dance, argue, kiss, drink, fight, joy ride and finally end up returning home at dawn. The film was intended to be a shocking exposé on the plight of these youngsters, but by today's standards,

Fig. 36

Fig. 37

Fig. 38

Fig. 39

Fig. 40

Fig. 41

Fig. 42

Fig. 43

Fig. 44

their "shabby" tenement seems rather quaint; their rough neighborhood, almost pleasant. [45-49]

Even "photographic evidence" purposely intended to demonstrate unacceptable standards is contradictory. Housing Authority captions are strewn with terms like "slum" and "blight," but what captures the eye are healthy children playing under lines of laundry, well-groomed families in neatly kept living rooms and senior citizens quietly resting on their porches.

In one scene from *The Exiles*, to express a character's desperate loneliness, a young woman walks home from downtown up dark stairs and through abandoned alleys. What affects us is not that she is lonely, but that she, otherwise, feels entirely comfortable.

People today don't use the hill at night. They park in subterranean garages, work, have lunch, return to work, then head home. They don't want to walk the long distances or climb the steps or cross the wide ramp or wait for the elevator because there is no reward. There is no winding path and no shady lawn, no little old lady feeding pigeons and no little old man asleep on the bench, no grove of trees dropping fruit and no rickety train rumbling overhead. Instead, sadly, there is a glass and steel projection of central power pasted atop a decapitated

Fig. 45

Fig. 46

hill—a high-modern corporate utopia yet to match any part of the rich mystique and organic excitement its predecessor embodied. Forced into a standardized form, the cast has cracked along with the mold.

After abandoning the myth of downtown "redevelopment," after tiring of the downtown "center vs. district" debate, after accepting that even in "sunny" Los Angeles, it is wiser to live with nature than try to subdue her, with what are we left? We are left with an expensive lesson. A lesson in patience, prejudice and arrogance. With the resurfacing of Broadway and the upcoming structural retrofitting of its historic buildings steadily approaching, we will soon find out how well we have learned it.

***

1Kevin Lynch, *The Image of the City* (Cambridge: M.I.T. Press, 1960), pg. 15.
2Ibid., 33.
3Ibid., 15. Lynch's study was based on interviews with local residents.
4Ibid., 36. "Bunker Hill is not as strong an image, despite its historical connotations, and quite a few felt that it was 'not in the downtown area.' Indeed, it is surprising how the core, in bending around this major topographic feature, has succeeded in visually burying it."
5The Red Car line during its time was rated the finest mass transit system in the nation.

6Average for Eastern Cities, but very high for Los Angeles. See Norman M. Klein, *20th Century Los Angeles-Power, Promotion and Social Conflict.* (Claremont: Regina Books, 1990), pg. 24.

7The City Council made an agreement with the agency to warehouse Angel's Flight and eventually reinstall it (promising in some cases to do so with in one year). Over thirty years later, a business group called the Bunker Hill Associates was required not only to finally reinstall Angel's Flight (which they did in 1996) but to build and operate a museum as well.

8Macy's Plaza was formerly Broadway Plaza whose parent company established one of the first department stores in the area.

9 Richard Longstreth, *City Center to Regional Mall-Architecture, the Automobile, and Retailing in Los Angeles, 1920-1950* (Cambridge, Massachusetts: M.I.T. Press, 1997), pg.11.

10Kevin Starr, *The Dream Endures-California Enters the 1940s* (New York: Oxford University Press, 1997), pp. 167-170.

11The Spanish Law of the Indies is described in John W. Reps, *Town Planning in Frontier America* (Princeton: Princeton University Press, 1969), pg. 64.

12Lieutenant E.O.C. Ord, "Los Angeles City Map No. 1/Plan de la Ciudad de Los Angeles", 1849.

13Maggie Valentine, *The Show Starts on the Sidewalk-An Architectural History of the Movie Theater* (New Haven: Yale University Press, 1994), pp. 17-18.

14Clunes's Broadway is now called the Cameo Theater. David Gebhard and Robert Winter, *Los Angeles-An Architectural Guide* (Salt Lake City: Gibbs Smith, 1994), pg. 235.

Fig. 47

Fig. 48

15The Pantages is now called The Arcade. David Gebhard and Robert Winter, *Los Angeles-An Architectural Guide* (Salt Lake City: Gibbs Smith, 1994), pg. 235.

16Ibid., 235-6.

17Some theaters restricted "colored seating" to balconies while others designated certain nights of the week for Black attendance, other nights for Latino attendance. Many hotels, restaurants and retailers would also practice discrimination. See Norman M. Klein, *20th Century Los Angeles-Power, Promotion and Social Conflict* (Claremont: Regina Books, 1990), pg. 105.

18Robert Mayer, *Los Angeles: A Chronological and Documentary History, 1542-1976* (Dobbs Ferry: Oceana Publications, 1978), pg. 73.

19For a description of the camp, see Jeane Houston Wakatsuki and James D. Houston, *Farewell To Manzanar* (New York: Bantam Pathfinder Editions, 1973).

20*Four Hundred-Fifty Years of Chicano History* (Albuquerque: Chicano Communications Center, 1976), pp. 106-107.

21Robert Mayer, *Los Angeles: A Chronological and Documentary History, 1542-1976* (Dobbs Ferry: Oceana Publications, 1978), pg. 76.

22Ibid., 76-77. This was the old MTA. Since then, this agency has changed identities numerous times. The present MTA receives State and Federal funding. It also receives funding from Proposition "A" and from its own revenues.

23Ibid, 78.

24 Some major chains such as the Gap and Footlocker

had moved out by that time.

25W.W. Robinson, *The Story of Pershing Square* (Los Angeles: Title Guarantee and Trust Company, 1931), pg. 15-16.

26The winning architects were SITE of New York.

27The use of bright colors and simple geometric forms are similar to the Riding School at San Cristobal, Mexico, 1962-8. Architect-Luis Barragán.

28In the early '80s, the B.H.A. and Arthur Erickson proposal for California Plaza had been chosen over the MacGuire Thomas Partners scheme. In the late '80s MacGuire Thomas rejected the winning Pershing Square design.

29Charles Moore, *Los Angeles-The City Observed* (New York: Vintage Books, 1984), pg. 4. "On the west side of the hill runs the Harbor Freeway; on the south side is the startlingly unprepossessing business and financial center of the western United States, fashioned of straight-up-and-down new buildings, rising without any ceremony at bottom or top to arbitrary and unpredictable heights, like so many random extrusions. The closest parallel is perhaps an asparagus patch, where the tallest stalk and the shortest are just alike, except that the tallest has shot farther out of the ground. The L.A. asparagus patch is particularly shiny."

30*The Exiles*, directed by Kent MacKenzie, 1961.

Fig. 49

Fig. 1

A Million Bricks A Day

Standing out on the Main Street Hotel fire escape, driving by the warehouses south of Sunset, meeting for drinks at a plush Hollywood Boulevard restaurant, searching through the bars on Central Avenue, buying a second-hand suit at the Goodwill on Broadway. Readers of Los Angeles literature can easily imagine the buildings in these scenes.[1] They are old buildings, brick buildings, old faded dusty brick buildings. [1-5]

In film, brick is the backdrop for urban scenes. In song, lyrics depict street life bordered by brick. Painters, photographers and poets all use brick to build their images and frame their ideas. When Bukowski has a fist fight, when Jim Morrison and Donna Summer cruise the Strip, when Gene Kelly sings in the rain, the background is brick.

Brick buildings line our commercial cor-

Fig. 2

Fig. 3

Fig. 4

Fig. 5

Fig. 6

Fig. 7

Fig. 8

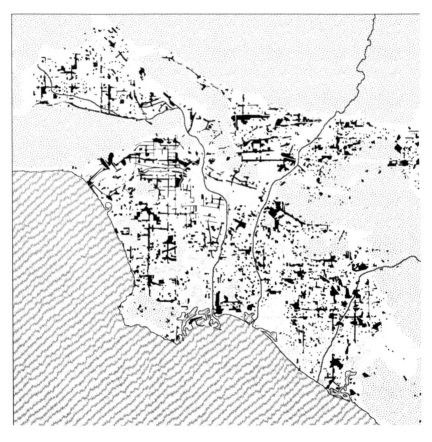

Commercial Corridors   Fig. 9

ridors—old, ordinary, brick buildings with one, two or perhaps several floors, an entrance on the sidewalk, a sign in front and merchandise in the display window. [6-8] These are the more mature buildings that comprise our city's skeleton.[2] [9] The cleaners, the corner drug, the neighborhood market, the pizza parlor, the roller rink, the ninety-nine cent store, the video rental. [10]

And beyond the railroad tracks, there are more. The auto parts supply, the tire repair, the garment factory, the lumber yard, the import/export business, the antique barn, the coffee house, the artist loft, the trendy restaurant, the small theater. Whether they're styled Egyptian Revival, Streamline Modern or English Tudor; [11-13] whether they have reflected mirror balls, full-size missles, checkerboard entrances, giant sunflower facades or mural scenes from Fiddler on the Roof; [14-17] whether they have been glazed, sandblasted or painted like a cow; [18-19] these are the buildings we constantly use, the buildings we spend much of our lives in. Buildings built before concrete, steel and glass were so easily manipulable. Brick buildings, old faded dusty cracking brick buildings.

Once our city was made of these buildings. Yes, a house could be wood and stucco,

Fig. 10

Fig. 11

Fig. 12

Fig. 13

Fig. 14

Fig. 15

Fig. 16

Fig. 17

Fig. 18

Fig. 19

but a building was brick. A house could be a dream, a show place or a humble bungalow, but a building had to be more substantial, more permanent. Together in rows brick buildings formed the anchor to the community, the town center, the Main Street. [20-22]

Architect Robert Venturi in his 1966 essay *Complexity and Contradiction in Architecture*[3] forced a rethinking of the treatment of our brick Main Streets. Architects, engineers, planners, and maybe even a developer or two began to reconsider their scorched earth schemes—maybe scores of buildings didn't need to be wiped away every time a new project came along. Maybe Main Street was worth preserving or even renovating. Maybe, "Main Street was almost alright."

In Los Angeles County, we have at least eleven named Main Streets. To us (like the old term, "Mission Road"), "Main Street" holds a more generic meaning. We crave the familiarity, security, pride and convenience our old commercial corridors once provided. And when we look at Main Street, Los Angeles; Main Street, Santa Monica; Main Street, Culver City; Main Street, Alhambra; Main Street, La Puente; Main Street, El Segundo... what do we see? Old buildings, brick buildings. Old faded dusty cracking brick buildings.

Fig. 20

Fig. 21

Fig. 22

In Los Angeles, we have planned and built ourselves into successive urban marvel and urban ruin. Over dismantled trolley tracks, our cars and freeways run roughshod upon our pedestrian and public transit lives. As early as 1961, Jane Jacobs in her critique *The Death and Life of Great American Cities* gave instructions for urban vitality. Almost forty years later, despite her warning, our malls, office buildings and shopping centers turn the street inside out, leaving our parking lots full and our sidewalks and wallets empty.

Fortunately though, after decades of trial and error, architects and urban planners have begun to pay their respects to the old dusty, cracking, peeling ordinary buildings on our main commercial corridors. Many now acknowledge the value of short blocks, wide sidewalks, new and old businesses, antique facades, narrow back alleys, small scale corridors and comprehensible entrances.[4] The scale and proportion of brick is back in style from Third to Ventura, the Boardwalk to Broadway, Melrose to Whittier. [23-24] And in Pasadena red brick has turned into green dollars. [25-31]

By purchasing easements to facades, Pasadena was able to upgrade an ordinary row of thrift shops, porno magazine stands and liquor stores into one of the most expensive dis-

Fig. 23

Fig. 24

Fig. 25

Fig. 26

Fig. 27

Fig. 28

Fig. 29

Fig. 30

Fig. 31

tricts in the county. Brick is not disguised but exposed. A red brick display room, a back alley dining patio, a neon entrance lobby, a wood-truss bar, these are simple understandable spaces—ordered, regular, predictable and pedestrian.

But not only in Pasadena. Much of our county is brick. Thousands upon thousands of buildings throughout downtown, Hollywood, Glendale, Burbank, Beverly Hills, Westwood, Santa Monica, Whittier, Inglewood, Alhambra, Van Nuys... On every major surface street: Sunset, Wilshire, Santa Monica, Pico, Olympic, Manchester, Ventura, Pacific Coast Highway, Greenleaf, Colorado, Vermont, Western, Central, Soto... They're in North Hollywood, Altadena, Sierra Madre, San Gabriel, El Monte, Vernon, Maywood, Bell, Watts, Hawthorne, Culver City, Pomona. Brick buildings—old, faded, dusty, cracking, peeling, run down—and now after 1988—retrofitted earthquake-resistant brick buildings. [32]

Earthquake?

Did someone say EARTHQUAKE!?!

Get away from that window! Duck under the table! Stand in the doorway!

But wait a minute--what about brick?

In 1994, even though Northridge was the epicenter of a major earthquake, we did not hear

Fig. 32

Fig. 33

Fig. 34

Fig. 35

a lot about old brick buildings collapsing as they had in San Francisco a few years before. Why? Because Los Angeles had been preparing since 1988. And how did a whole county keep a force that collapsed several freeways, toppled modern offices, and sandwiched apartment houses left and right from sweeping aside a bunch of sixty and seventy year old piles of brick?

Have you, by any chance, seen little six-inch steel plates and heavy duty steel moment frames in the middle of your favorite restaurant, coffee house or Laundromat? Rows of anchor bolts, concrete block in-filled windows and cement – buttressed walls have done their job. These aggregate bandages and steel sutures have quietly snuck into our lives. [33-35] Ten years after mandating the Earthquake Hazard Reduction Ordinance (Division 88) of the Los Angeles Municipal Building Code, the city can breathe a sigh of relief that its seismic program was carried out and its valuable more mature brick buildings have had years added to their lives. We can be proud of these threads and needles of iron and embrace them as part of our city and its natural shaky nervousness.

Now, despite their recent accomplishments, these buildings are not big show-offs. They are small, simply organized and more similar than varied. Critics often describe our city

Fig. 36

as monotonous, repetitive and uniform. Published descriptions include: "formless," "spread out," "without centers," "...scatter and amplitude of open space", "monotony, not unity," "an inhabited fragment of the desert."[5] But uniformity, repetition and even monotony have their place. The beautiful cities of Mijas and Villa Hermosa in Spain, Pisticci in Italy and Khartoum in the Sudan consist of buildings that to our eyes are indistinguishable one from another. Farmhouses in Cisternino, Victorian facades in San Fransisco and the town square arcade of Telc, Czechoslovakia all use uniformity and repetition to give order to public space.

Locally, in groups, brick buildings perform much the same tasks. They provide rhythm and grounding to a neighborhood. They define the sidewalk and give local identity. They mark places from which the city grew.

Local regulations limited height so although Unreinforced Masonry Buildings (URMs) come in many sizes, their designs are conservative and follow simple rules. Generally they are limited to a half a dozen stories without a steel or concrete frame, and a dozen stories with one. In any case, locally, they never go above 150 feet tall. [36-37]

Generally, a one-story URM perimeter wall is thirteen inches wide to allow for a row of

Fig. 37

Fig. 38

bricks turned cross-ways. [38] In two-story buildings, an additional layer makes the lower wall seventeen inches. Taller buildings required thicker ground floor walls while upper floors were kept as thin as nine inches or constructed of lighter materials such as wood and stucco.

Decorative treatments might include relief pediments, column fretwork, corner molding and corbeled window sills. [39-43] Parapets often have a concrete cap or a row of glazed brick at the cornice. Stepping parapets generally appear on the sides and backs of buildings, but occasionally they appear on the front, peaking ceremonially in the center. [44-45]

Roofs most commonly consist of ship's trusses, carpenter's trusses or simple post and beam construction. Ship's trusses generally rest on engaged columns while carpenter's trusses are repeated as closely as two to four feet apart. Skylights are common, especially in larger buildings to allow light into the center of the space. [46-47]

Openings are limited in size and proportion, occasionally arching, but in general having lintels of steel or concrete. Although the openings in some elevations today might appear randomly spaced due to alterations, architects generally spaced openings symmetrically either in

Fig. 39

Fig. 40

200

Fig. 41

Fig. 42

Fig. 43

Fig. 44

Fig. 45

204

Fig. 46

Fig. 47

relation to the front entrance or in relation to the columns. [48-50]

Ground floors and foundations are typically concrete slabs. If the ground floor falls below grade, it is often expressed as a socle or pedestal. Ironwork, keystones and other more elaborate ornamentation is not uncommon especially on office blocks and movie palaces.

Interior spaces are generally singular with a strong sense of closure and a feeling of security. [51] These spaces are clearly organized and generally relate directly to the street. Display windows are generally symmetrical, scaled for the pedestrian, and oriented to the sidewalk. [52-53]

Other characteristics also make brick buildings appropriate to the Southern California landscape. They are fire-resistant, carry sufficient mass to keep interior temperatures comfortable, sturdy enough to absorb minor ground motion and resilient enough to sustain dry heat, gusty wind and torrential downpour. Their flat roofs are consistent with a region free of snow.

Brick buildings also fitted in well with the strict code and layout of early Los Angeles.[6] The city's first brick dwelling was La Casa Pelanconi built in 1855.[7] After the shift away from adobe and the building booms of the late 1800s, the demand for brick expanded exponen-

Fig. 48

Fig. 49

Fig. 50

Fig. 51

Fig. 52

Fig. 53

tially. By 1912, local kilns were producing one million bricks a day.[8] But after the 1933 Long Beach earthquake left over one hundred people dead, regulations were passed requiring steel reinforcing when brick was used structurally.

The Modern Movement called for the use of new materials and for the elimination of even the modest ornament that URM buildings exhibited. But unlike Victorian houses, URMs were flexible enough to survive post-war trends. With the increased dependence on the auto, URMs were even plastered over with huge superscale signage to compete with the new shopping centers. Many have been altered beyond recognition. [54-59] Various others are simply hidden behind layers of veneer.

One example is in Maywood—a plain facade hides a cleaning supply factory at 4535 East Slauson. In this case, conflicting needs drove the front entrance to the back and internalized the building's most expressive aspects. A simple grid within a perfect square in plan, this building, filled with chemicals, has withdrawn itself from the street. [60-62]

While some URMs were disguised, others were preserved. A fine example of a well-preserved URM is 2328 Santa Fe Avenue which sits on the edge of a streetlightless semi-public industrial zone south of downtown. Its design is

Fig. 54

Fig. 55

Fig. 56

Fig. 57

Fig. 58

Fig. 59

symmetrical and well-proportioned with two bays facing west and eight bays facing south. It is a border building; a cornerpost between two zones, elegantly ornamenting the entrance to an industrial district. [63-67]

A more work-a-day example of an altered URM is 2433 Hunter Street, a warehouse on a two block cul-de-sac on the southern shore of the 10 Freeway. The rhythms of the middle and upper parts of its front facade tie 2433 to its neighbors while accommodating backing trucks. Its back is sealed off from abandoned railroad tracks and the arrangement of its contents complies well with the organization of columns in plan and skylights on the roof. Predecessor to the 10 Freeway by more than two decades, 2433 Hunter Street remains active and well adjusted to its new purveyor. [68-70]

Of course not all URMs survived. The Division 88 requirements created a sort of do or die period. If owners could not afford to retrofit, they had to demolish. Earthquakes and fires exacerbated the situation. An example of a building that did not make it and was razed during this period was 645 East Washington Boulevard which once occupied the entire northwest corner of San Pedro Street and East Washington Boulevard. A large apartment building--its involution of corridors served as

Fig. 60

Fig. 61

221

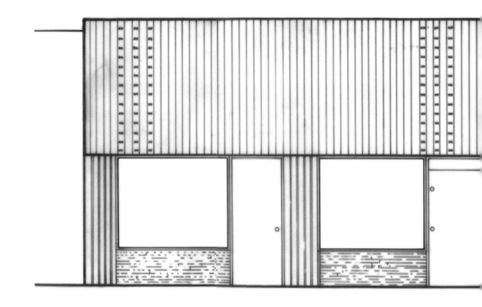

4535-9 East Slauson Bl.

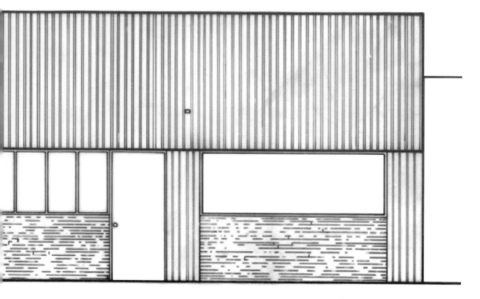

SOUTH ELEVATION

Fig. 62

Fig. 63

Fig. 64

Fig. 65

Fig. 66

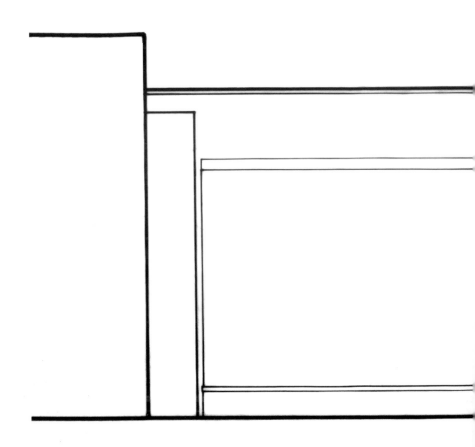

2328 South Santa Fe Ave.

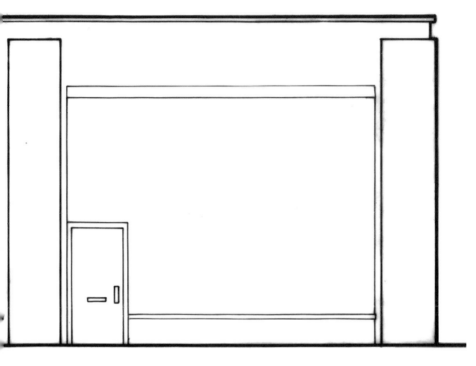

WEST ELEVATION

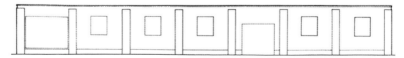

SOUTH ELEVATION

Fig. 67

Fig. 68

Fig. 69

Fig. 70

play space. Over the years, hundreds of children stretched their growing legs running and playing up and down the long halls. The compact units in more recent times sufficed as low-income housing during successive periods of neglectful ownership and apathetic public authority. It was demolished in March 1991. [71-80]

Perhaps most importantly, URMs help us recognize where we live. We identify with them. They are consistent and stable—a link to our past. They give us a sense of our place--one that Christian Norburg-Schulz might describe as a "Cosmic Landscape." A landscape that does not contain individual places, but forms a "continuous neutral ground."[9] Saving the URMs was valuable not only for the safety and structural improvements but also for the opportunity to form an indigenous set of buildings within marginal streets and districts. Alone and together the URMs with their shared new markings, reach out to the city while holding onto the landscape.

***
—

1These scenes are from the work of the following authors: Joan Didion, Budd Schulberg, Walter Mosley, Raymond Chandler and John Fante.
2 Commercial Corridors Map after Michael W. Donley,

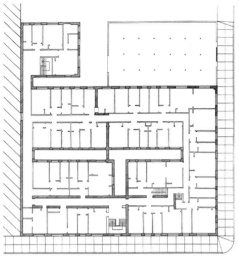

SECOND FLOOR PLAN

FIRST AND THIRD SIMILAR

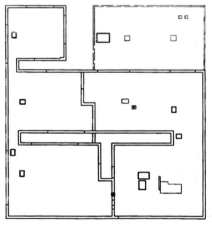

ROOF PLAN

645 East Washington Blvd.

Fig. 71

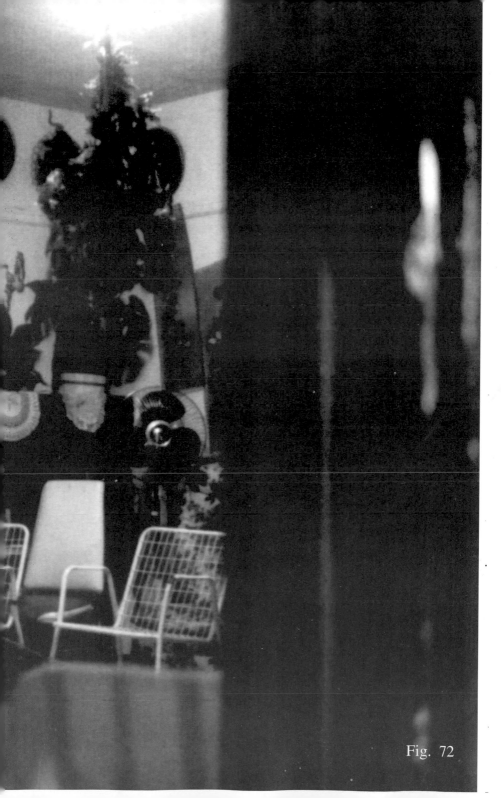

Fig. 72

Fig. 73

Fig. 74

Fig. 75

Fig. 76

Fig. 77

Fig. 78

Fig. 79

Fig. 80

Atlas of California (Culver City: Pacific Book Center, 1979).

3Robert Venturi, *Complexity and Contradiction in Architecture* (New York: Museum of Modern Art, 1966), pg. 104.

4Jane Jacobs, *The Death and Life of Great American Cities* (New York: Vintage Books, 1961).

5These are quotes from Jane Jacobs, Reyner Banham, Kevin Lynch, and, Jean Baudrillard, *America.* (New York: Verso, 1988).

6John W. Reps, *Town Planning in Frontier America* (Princeton: Princeton University Press, 1969), pg. 64.

7David Gebhard and Robert Winter, *Los Angeles-An Architectural Guide* (Salt Lake City: Gibbs-Smith Publisher, 1994), pg. 251.

8Robert Mayer, *Los Angeles: a chronological and documentary history, 1542-1976* (Dobbs Ferry, New York: Oceana Publication, Inc. 1978).

9Christian Norberg-Schulz, *Genius Loci-Towards a Phenomenology of Architecture* (New York: Rizzoli, 1980).

Unreinforced Masonry Studio
P.O. Box 33671
Los Angeles, CA   90033